Praise for *Mitmensch*

"*Mitmensch* is Corey Mesler's natural tale-spinning ability in miniature, emblazoned on pages that expected just another book of poetry. As always, he surprises in the best of ways— his unconventional style changes pillowed between poems that turn on his unique use of metaphor. *Mitmensch* was surprising and unexpected and lovely and filthy and right and wrong and I loved it."

~Jessica Dawson, author of *Fossil Fuels*

"In this series of linked poems, Mesler paints a portrait of an Everyman: Mitmensch, who 'knows there is feeling here somewhere' in these lives that are like 'a message that never gets through.' He 'was once a god among bugs' but now is trying to convince his coworkers he's a genius. He's 'hungry for…a little more of everything.' Mesler shows us again why he's one of the most widely published writers out there."

~CL Bledsoe, author of *Man of Clay* and *The Saviors*

"Mesler is one of the truly unique voices of our time... like a slide-guitar Browning, he addresses the reader personally, and you will listen. I find myself getting lost in the metaphors, at first deceptively simple but in the end profound...and true."

~Ward Abel, author of *Cousins over Colder Fields*
and *American Bruise*

"Whether he's reporting from the bowels of the Piggly Wiggly or the capacious birthing canal of an alien on the planet Sniff, the lambent haecceity of Corey Mesler never fails to shine through time and space and the sulfurous stench of the human heart. We are all Mitmensch."

~Linda Heck, singer-songwriter, whose latest
CD is entitled *Transformed*

MITMENSCH

Corey Mesler

Happy holidays,
2015.

Corey

MITMENSCH

Corey Mesler

FOLDED WORD

Rocklin

ISBN-13: 978-1-61019-906-3

Folded Word
5209 Del Vista Way
Rocklin, CA 95765
United States of America
www.foldedword.com

Cover and Design by J.S. Graustein
Titles set in Berlin Sans FB, text in Adobe Caslon Pro
Printed in the United States of America, United Kingdom, and Australia

For Cheryl, Toby and Chloe
and for my brother, Mark and my sister, Sue

MITMENSCH

"His mind burned like a flame but his heart stank of sulphur."

~Frederick Prokosch

WHERE MITMENSCH CAME FROM

Mitmensch comes from humble beginnings.
He comes from humble beginnings.
When a child, his mother would marvel at his
innate ability to conjure bullydom.
And his artistic leanings, his artistic leanings
sparkled, connecting all around him.
She was so proud of him. And when he lost
contest after contest, when frustration
set in like a flu, she marveled anew at the
rage he could invoke. Mitmensch
wanted only to be an artist. An artist. And,
failing that, his restless energies
moved on. They moved on to other cogencies,
his ovens, his makeshift ditches, his ditches.

MITMENSCH AS CAPORAL

Mitmensch walks the halfmile to
his place of work.
Today his employees will tempt him
verily, tempt him
to declare that he is a superman.
Mitmensch will exercise
his supreme will power—he will
bring to bear
upon the circumstances the righteous
control of the deathless.
And he will sleep tonight, our Mitmensch,
wrapped in hungry dreams,
dreams about the end of the world, and
afterwards the manifold possibilities.

MITMENSCH IN LOVE

O how his heart sang, his cinereous heart!
O how his love smiled when they met,
his plucky gill!
And when they bedded, O people,
the sweet fireworks,
the torn screams of pleasure, the reckless
flight from terra firma.
O Mitmensch, that is your heart engaging,
your tried, tired heart!
Sing out for our hero, Mitmensch! O how
he loves,
how he goes after her like prey, how his
fingers sink into her,
how his eyes devour her! O Mitmensch,
how he owns his love!

MITMENSCH WOBBLING

Mitmensch feels a fool
today, the morning
a bubble, a
ragged accordion.
Mitmensch knows there
is feeling here
somewhere, children,
wildings, a wife,
a hank of hair.
But Mitmensch is low,
thinking black
thoughts, trembling where
he formerly
scrapped like a cat.
Mitmensch was once a god
among bugs.
Those days are fragile
like a kite,
the string unraveling, the
string unraveling.
Mitmensch makes it to the
threshold, where
he holds steady. The light
is just beyond him,
the tremulous light.
Mitmensch is returning,

slowly refilling
his tanks, hungry for more,
a little more
of everything.

LIVING NEAR MITMENSCH

The pistol's cocked.
The end table is the living end.
Mitmensch sits so still
the neighbors think he is dead.
This is their first mistake.
The snake is for later.
The mickeyed drink is what is
offered. The party flags.
Mitmensch rises slowly, like a
uniform unfolding.
The neighbors start to salute.
This is their next mistake.

Our Relation to Mitmensch

Mitmensch, student of the known,
how came you to this state,
this unwieldy power?
In your younger days did you break
pigeons onetwothree?
Make a salad of your correspondence?
Speak the last word
when the last word was called for?
We have so many questions, Mitmensch,
we who dangle along
like a song that won't end, like a message
that never gets through.
We mark time with a chalkstick, believing
that the sidewalk goes around the world.
Mitmensch, our benefactor!

Ventripotent Mitmensch

In middle age Mitmensch became ventripotent.
He did not like the protuberance;
no he was just vain enough to find in it a deep
sadness. So, he redoubled his efforts
in his business, stepping on lesser men, one, two,
three, and, in this way, felt better about
his appearance. And, let's face it, women came
to him at all hours—power, money,
these were aphrodisiacs. A rounded middle only
mattered to the middle and lower classes.

Mitmensch

What's his name?

> His name?

That's what I'm asking.

> You wanna know his name.

I do.

> He said to wait here.

I know. You said that. I'd like to know who
we're talking about.

> He's a guy.

Just a guy.

> No, he ain't just any guy.

But you can't divulge his name.

> Mitmensch, his name is Mitmensch.

Just Mitmensch.

That's all I know.

But, presumably, he has more than one name.
Presumably he does. We think that.

Yes.

This Mitmensch. This guy. He only told you
one name.

That's the score.

And he said to wait here.

Yes.

Mitmensch, this guy, this guy who you don't
even know his whole name, said to wait here
and, so we're here.

Obviously, we're here.

Waiting.

Yes.

Did he say what the cut was?

The cut?

10

Right. I assume you know to ask what the
cut is.

                              I didn't. Ask.

For fug sake.

              Look, he was presented to me as someone
                  we could trust, a straight-up guy. Not
                      just any guy, a straight-up guy, with
                                              connections.

And so we wait.

                                              Yes.

For how long?

                  I was told it wouldn't take long.

The job?

                                       The wait.

The wait wouldn't take long?

                                       Right.

To find out the job.

11

That's right. That's what Mitmensch said.

I follow.

                                                      Ok.

Tell me one thing.

                                              What's that?

This Mitmensch, this guy who didn't discuss
cuts, he's connected you say? So the job is,
presumably, legit?

                                    That's what I presume.

Ok.

                                  That all you need to know?

I needed to know why I'm waiting.

                                      Ok. We square now?

Yes. I'll wait.

                                                    Good.

The cut better be equitable.

12

Equitable. This is what you need. An
equitable cut.

> That's what I need, yes. That's what buys
> my involvement.

Ok.

> Me and you. You told him it was two of
> us. That the cut would involve two of us.

Yes.

> You told Mitmensch this?

That's right.

> Ok.

⧗

> The job is simple. The job is forthright.
> No two faces under one hood, ask
> anyone. This isn't the beginning, friends,
> this isn't a virgin voyage. You follow me,
> we all make good. I need straight-up
> guys, guys with blood. You got blood,

you follow me, we all do the job. We do the job and we make good. I'm no mook; I'm a safe card, right? You know from what you hear. You hear about me; that's good. That's what I want; you hear about me. I was told two guys, two guys with blood. This what we have? Blood in their veins, you know me? I'm telling you the job is a good job, a proper job; you follow? And when it's done, when the job is jobbed, we're jimmies, you got me? It's simple, like a nun's prayer. We go home on the pig's back. I was told two guys. You right with me?

We're two.

Right.

And the job, its—

The job is what it is. The job is what we do.

Ok.

And you got the blood? Both of you?

Right.

This one doesn't talk. You a colt? Guys
that don't talk make me nervous.

I talk.

Ok, then.

I got blood.

I see that. Ok? You say so; I see it.
That's what I am, straight-up.

Ok.

Listen, Mitmensch—

I'm here.

The split, we didn't talk the split.

You worry about the split up front?

Yeah.

That's good. That's right. You get that
up front, the details, what we call the
distinctiveness of the job.

Right.

You get the split, the even split. I tell
you, I'm good, right? I tell you, I'm no
mook.

Yes, sir.

Ok. You get the split, whatcha call it?
Moiety.

Ok.

You still talking?

I talk.

Good. We're good, then. We do the
job, we're right; ok? We're jimmies.

Ok.

Good.

That was ok then, right? You ok?

                                    Yeah, sure.

He's ok. Right? He's good.

                                    Yeah, he's good.

You're saying good?

                                         Yes.

We're ok then.

                              He has a—what?

Swagger?

                                         No.

Charisma? Charm?

                    No. A, damn, what's the word?

I don't know where you're going.

                    He's—monumental. No, that's not
                                        the word.

Imposing.

That's better.

August.

Ok.

Skookum.

I don't know.

Anyway, we're good to go. You feel good
about this?

Yeah. Sure.

We won't get our combs cut, right?

Sure.

We're out of collar, otherwise.

Out of collar.

That's what I'm saying.

Yes.

This Mitmensch, this guy. He's A-one. He's
no buzzard, right?

                                        Sure.

I'll follow him. For the cut. He's a collector.

                          For the cut. Yes.

Ok.

                                      Listen.

I'm here.

                    I'm, you know, I'm in. I'm way in.

Uh huh.

                                          Pal.

Yeah.

                          I'm scared to death.

Scared.

                                         Yes.

Scared to death.

                                        Yes.

Ok.

                                    It's ok.

Yes.

                          I'm scared to death.

Me, too. I'm scared to death, too.

MITMENSCH THERE NEAR THE END

Mitmensch continued his bloody run.
We citizens stayed indoors.
The world was his to rape if his desires
ran in that direction.
His desires always did.
When Gayla became my wife I understood
that the day might come
when Mitmensch would take her away.
I understood that if there
were children, they too were stopgap.
So, when the air turned livid and
the lakes dried up
I thought that it was time to turn to my wife
and offer her my only plea.
I said, Gayla, when Mitmensch comes
let me keep a nest of birds,
a small nest of birds.
It's comforting now, in this city of ash,
to watch them try to fly,
spreading their little oily wings, almost
cheeping, their eggs cold
black stones, their dying so slow and elegant.

MITMENSCH ENDGAME

His head like a pile of plates.
His shifting geography.
His way of talking that is
not talking. His silences.
His beautiful hands, the
way he uses them.
His eye, his vision, his face,
as open as melting charity.
His legacy, how we talk.
And the endless ink like
blood, leading us inward and
then back to the beginning.
In our beginnings, our way.
That is all I have to say,
at this time, about Mitmensch.

About the Author

COREY MESLER has published in numerous journals and anthologies. He has published six novels, *Talk: A Novel in Dialogue* (2002), *We Are Billion-Year-Old Carbon* (2006), *The Ballad of the Two Tom Mores* (2010), *Following Richard Brautigan* (2010), *Gardner Remembers* (2011), and *Frank Comma and the Time-Slip* (2012); two full length poetry collections, *Some Identity Problems* (2008) and *Before the Great Troubling* (2011); and three books of short stories, *Listen: 29 Short Conversations* (2009), *Notes Toward the Story and Other Stories* (2011) and *I'll Give You Something to Cry About* (2011). He has also published a dozen chapbooks of both poetry and prose. He has been nominated for the Pushcart Prize numerous times, and two of his poems have been chosen for Garrison Keillor's *Writer's Almanac*. His fiction has received praise from John Grisham, Robert Olen Butler, Lee Smith, Frederick Barthelme, and Greil Marcus, among others. With his wife, he runs Burke's Book Store in Memphis TN, one of the country's oldest (1875) and best independent bookstores. He can be found at:

COREYMESLER.WORDPRESS.COM

Acknowledgements

The author would like to thank the staff of the following journals for publishing previous versions of the poems listed below:

"Mitmensch" in *Stranger Box*
"Mitmensch in Love" in *Stick your Neck Out*
"Where Mitmensch Came From" in *Typewriter Voodoo*
"Mitmensch Wobbling" in *Tryst*

The publishers would also like to thank Liana Gott, Kurt Graustein, and Miran Reynolds for their editorial assistance during the production of this book.

For a complete list of our titles plus multi-media presentations from this book, visit the Folded Word website: WWW.FOLDEDWORD.COM

To report typographical errors or problems with the functionality of this chapbook, email EDITORS@FOLDEDWORD.COM

Want more information about our books, chapbooks, and zines? Want to connect with contributors from this book? No problem. Simply join us at a social media outlet near you:

   weblog: FOLDED.WORDPRESS.COM
   Facebook: WWW.FACEBOOK.COM/FOLDEDWORD
   Twitter: TWITTER.COM/FOLDEDWORD
   YouTube: WWW.YOUTUBE.COM/USER/FOLDEDWORD

We love to hear from our readers. If you give us feedback on MITMENSCH, we'll send you a free e-copy. Just send your thoughts via email to editors@foldedword.com with the subject line "MITMENSCH Feedback."

Cheers!

More from the Folded Family